BLUE FOR OCEANS

Charles Douthat

December 2010
For Ira —
One heart to another
Chis

Published by NHR Books

Copyright © 2010 Charles Douthat

Book design by Nicholas Rock
Cover design by Elsa Chiao
Cover art: John Constable, *Seascape Study with Rain Clouds,* 1827,
Royal Academy of Arts, image copyright Zenodat Verlagsgesellschaft

ISBN: 978-0-9829008-1-9

Printed in the United States of America

NHR Books are available from www.newhavenreview.com.

NHR Books is the book publishing arm of New Haven Literistic, Inc.,
the nonprofit publisher of the New Haven Review
(www.newhavenreview.com). Support from private foundations, corporate
giving programs, government programs, and generous individuals
helps make our public programs and the publication of our journal and
books possible. We gratefully acknowledge their support.
For more information contact us at editor@newhavenreview.com.

I

MENDOCINO   15

AMONG TREES   16

MADE   17

SCENT OF MELON   18

A WEDDING POEM   19

THE POLISHINGS   20

PART OF THE PLEASURE   22

GREEN   23

FIRST HOUR   24

ON THE SCALE   25

ABOUT THE SNOW   26

SOMETIMES AT NIGHT I PRAY FOR MY COUNTRY   27

OUR YEAR   28

GOING ON THIS WAY LIVING FOREVER   30

THE HOLD   32

II

OUR VILLANELLE   37

THIS WRECK   38

HARVEST   40

WINTER HILL   41

BLESSED ARE THOSE WHO REMEMBER   42

LABOR DAY   43

CHINA   44

MRS. MILLER   45

COLD   46

THIS IS (HOW) TODAY   47

CRYING MAN   48

BEAUTIFUL BIRDS   49

THE LEAVES   50

III

FIVE MILES   55

AT THE HALL'S HOUSE   56

IN NOVEMBER   58

THE LIFE   59

THE MOVE   60

PASSAGE   61

4/11/02   62

STALK OF GRASS   64

MIDLIFE HAIKU   65

SPENT   66

ANOTHER SONG FOR MY FATHER   67

RACCOON   68

AT THE LAKE   69

BLUE FOR OCEANS   70

For Ross and Jeanne

I

Mendocino

The sun was hot in the place we loved.
Remember the grass and the sun right on us?
How it bore down! And the feeling of breathing
under glass. Each expression magnified.
Each sense focused. Edges browning, curling,
ready to burn. Then the first pale flames rising.
And you in the field in that lovely dress!
Summer-colored. Buttons up the back.
Those dark stockings with the sexy runs.
And no coat for cover or blanket under us.
O you were fine and the grass green and long.
But so hot. Almost painful. The blades cutting.
And sun in the grass so sweetly crushed.
And your legs moving like parts of me.
And love, on its knees in the grass
promising to remember us.

Among Trees

We were talking one day in winter.
I was speaking dispiriting things.
My teacher sighed.
Half turning in his chair, he looked out
the broad plate window toward the great pines.
Then, evenly, he began to speak.
First of an intractable shortcoming of his own.
Then of a heedless act regretted his whole life.
Past him through the glass, I could see beyond
the room's warm reflections.
Snow smoothed the ground. A lawn chair
left out from summer stood among real trees.

For W.S.

Made

Without knowing, we become.
Like a word mispronounced.
Or a screen door slammed.
Soup slowly burning
to the bottom of a pan.
First one thing, then another.
Among other things, we are.
Desired. Defaced. Discarded.
Yet generally ready for more.
We are sunlight in a window
and the glass within its frame.
We are the long view taken in
and a crack, barely visible
in the corner of the pane.
We are useful at times.
Or worse than useless.
Breakable. Beautiful. Made.

Scent of Melon

Let sorrow always greet me
as you greeted me at your door that day.
Like an old friend. And with a kiss.
And on the mouth, for once. Directly.
As earlier on the phone you'd said
"Always better to know."

Together we cleared the table
of half-wrapped fruit baskets,
get-well cards, sets of boxed herb teas
your patients had sent over. Then we talked—
sunlight's morning edge on the kitchen floor.

I drank coffee, ate cantaloupe, asked questions.
Like a hat, your wig hung on the next chair.
Explaining about lymph nodes
and the distances a bad cell can travel
you touched yourself to show how far.
"Here to here," you said. "Sometimes here."

So our kitchen talk went on.
Sunlight reached the table. Momentarily
the scent of melon was in the air.
And when you felt I knew enough
the conversation turned other ways.

Your son's new middle school.
My daughter giving up her dance.
Our last trips to the coast.
And then, while there was still time,
other friends and days.

For C.M.

A Wedding Poem

Pressured, we finally split, traveled East to wed.
Your dress, tissued in a suitcase, flew off with you

while I drove through fourteen over-heated August states.
At your parents' Maine coast cape I met them both.

Your pacing, ash-faced father abruptly quit the room.
Your mother stayed, chatting me up and down.

How restlessly I slept those nights before wedding.
The worn sheets smelling of bleach and ocean damp.

And beyond a peeling, antique wall, I seemed to hear
your childhood in the next room. That week I paid

two dollars for a license. Confused the family priest
with my religion. Thought the watered countryside small.

Your dress I'd forgotten until the afternoon before
when gunning up the gravel drive from town

I saw the windy, swinging shape of it, like a spirit
clothes-pinned to your mother's line. Against your wishes

she'd washed and shrunk it. Just a little, she claimed.
A part of you was bitter on our wedding day.

I remember your mother dancing with my best man.
The motel room your father reserved. And those first

raw altered hours. Talking and not. Your dress crumpled
on a bedside chair. The single window that didn't open.

The Polishings

In the warm painted porch
of our old stucco house
at the legged laundry sink
covered with a plywood board
my father taught me as a boy
as he'd been taught, how a salesman
ought to polish his good shoes.

"Make them shine enough to speak,"
he insisted. "They're your first step
through the door." He'd spread out
newspaper, rags and brushes
and metal tins that twisted open
with a pop, revealing creams—
deep brown, black, cordovan.

He taught me by doing: the rag
doubled to keep the gob of polish
from bleeding through;
the non-master hand like a foot
inside the worked-on shoe
to hold it steady; the thorough
coating and spreading over leather

of waxy color, starting from scuffed toe
then down the instep side to heel
and back to toe. Once both shoes
were creamed over, he lit a cigarette
to let the glazed pair dry. Hurried
brushing, he'd say, made a short-lived
shine that wouldn't last half a day

of cold calls on the road. My father
knew so much in his handsome hands—
gilded with a rectangled wristwatch
a wedding band, and between knuckles,
wiry sprays of golden hair.
I can still see one good hand hidden
inside a brogue, the other gripping

the wooden brush as it bristled out
a leathered glow. How long did they last
those lessons on the porch? One year?
Two? How long the morning polishings
with the jobless day before him
and a son watching, a wife waiting
and no door but ours to walk through.

Part of the Pleasure

Afterwards it was pleasant to feel legs separate
and see the air in their hotel room as brocade or fine linen.

Earlier, when the desk clerk rang with a business call
for the husband, the wife blithely answered, "Nobody here

by that name." Even earlier, as a prop, he'd bought
cigarettes from the machine in the lobby, though both

quit smoking years before. Eventually, sunlight angled
down from the blinds in their room, beamed off

a mirror table, reflected a wobbled crown of light
up to the ceiling. "How I feel," she said, pointing

at the liquid, wavering light. Already he was losing again
in pieces the feeling that she was central. He'd never

grown accustomed to the flux. Soon, where the sheets
pulled loose, she noticed her feet touching his ankle.

Then dozing off, he drooled on the pillow and talked
in his sleep about California as he often did.

She didn't wake him. Later, when he asked
what foolish things were said, she invented a dream,

a sexy one about his mother to make him laugh.
"Thanks for listening," he said. And when they started

to wrestle and kiss again, each tasted that tempered part
which is pleasure rising out of happiness while it lasts.

Green

Some days I walk down the street
where we lived and the fat man
who stole tomatoes
sits under the same old sycamore
tapping out his angry rhythms
on the knotted roots. And though
the children are no longer ours,
the oaks are no less generous
to the sidewalks with their shade.
Overhead, sweet air still arrives
through many simple branches—
some reaching skyward for joy,
others downcast for a reason.
We were like good trees
the years we lived on this street.
We were so green. Fresh as leaves.
And the days whispered through us.

First Hour

With the first child finally born
a nurse wrapped him in a stained sheet.
She was leaving the room to wash
and weigh him, to prick one pink heel
and squeeze for blood. Quickly then
the young man had to decide.
Go with his son for the satisfaction.
Or stay with a torn and empty wife.
It was his first full glimpse of freedom.
The broken water on the floor.
The toweled tray of used instruments.
A door opening to a hospital of doors.

On the Scale

One night when I was eight and asleep
the small economies were delivered to our house.

Whatever darkness brought them took back in trade
big pieces of my early family life.

Gone were sit-down restaurants, weekly movies
the ironing lady from the afternoons.

And with them went the joking atmosphere
from our dinner table, fresh-cut flowers,

the better cuts of meat. Saturdays at the market
my mother drew me to the deep end

of the butcher's case, where mounds of chuck
and chicken parts were mounted on the scale

for all to see. How I watched the red arrow
fly up and past the true weight, then fall

as my mother figured where the dial would stop,
where we would, and secretly if she had enough.

About the Snow

A winter night is stubborn, dark and slow.
At dusk the frozen sky is falling white.
What can we do about the snow?

The sleeper's head grows restless in the flow.
This dreaming cold will often lead to fright.
A winter night is stubborn, dark and slow.

The mind lies still until it starts to blow.
On roofs the drifts are gusted left and right.
What can we do about the snow?

The air is ice no blaze can warm and so
each window sends a chill, however slight.
A winter night is stubborn, dark and slow.

The crooked road we're made to follow
isn't clear. The plow is passing out of sight.
What can we do about the snow?

This cold goes deeper than we know.
And though we rage against our winter plight
the nights are no less stubborn, dark and slow.
What can we do about the snow?

Sometimes at Night I Pray for My Country

Now that I must go on living in a mighty country
I notice the stale iron smell
in a glass of water
and through attic windows
white clouds in their discouraged shapes.
Dogs often bark on the street
but only because they know me.
And last night after prayer I dreamed
of a small woman I once loved.
She was crying and holding out a newspaper
open to the obituaries.
The beautiful bones inside her fingers
were pointing out each tiny lettered word.
She said they were all children.
Our children. She began reading names.
There were dozens.
There were thousands.
Few were Americans.
Yet each one bore my good name.

Our Year

Still, there is hope this fading year
that next year will be our year

for a winter hike to the island quarry.
After the holidays, I'd propose.

In January, when dormant hardwoods
clatter in the wind and only a stray spruce

or cardinal lives for color. At such times
the quarry sleeps ice-locked

beneath sifting skins of snow. If it's safe
and thick enough, I'll take you out

across the ice to that spot
we swam those summers ago.

We'll walk again on water, solid now
beneath our feet. And I'll scrape clean

a snow-window for staring down
the frozen mirror of the deep.

Maybe only sealed off fissures.
Or rising bubbles captured in blue.

At least we'll see two bundled faces
looking back. And even so close to longest

night, surely some remnant sun will flash
above the trees and find us there—

parchment-lit, in the open—and stir us
in a winter way we've never known.

Then let the sun flash on across our quarry.
Love, let it glitter in the quarry stone.

Going on this Way Living Forever

Before the betrayal were the years on Bradley Street.
Those lovely, lonely, stupid years with only odd jobs
and borrowed money and deep winters
we walked through happily together.

Always we were arriving early or at the very latest
on time, knowing no one in town yet
and having nowhere to go but the Italian corner market
where the owner gave us soft plums for the baby

and nectarines that spurted and juiced down his chins.
Our flat was below the turnpike and behind a hill.
Even the television reception was poor. Yet tomorrow
arrived each morning before breakfast, and yesterday left us

always with the rich taste of starting out in our mouths.
Most afternoons there was mail to wait for.
Having nothing, we were always expecting something.
The least little card or advertisement excited us

as if to those few, bright, thrift-store furnished rooms
a future would soon be brilliantly delivered.
No one could go on this way living forever.
Evenings, I started slipping out with my notebooks

to the old stone library on Elm Street.
In the main reading room, near racked magazines
I'd sit at one end of a long scarred table, penciling out plans,
gauging my own reactions. From the high blistered ceiling

paint chips drifted down like leaves. I considered
every option. Leave you and the baby. Take my ambition
back to California or on to New York alone.
But one day I spent half our rent on three dress shirts

and a blue suit at Sears. I threw out my notebooks
and for a year that rolled over me like a wheel
I'd jack up the car stereo and shout out Springsteen's
Thunder Road on my way to work.

Darling, no one was listening.
No one will ever care about our lives as we did.
You must say what's carried you through.
For myself, I call it betrayal now

only out of this battered gratitude.
But for the lost days and their beauty
how would we know to recover?
What would we have to mourn?

The Hold

There it is! Just before putting out the light.
Here in the doorway to his room.
The unmistakable smell of him,
though his train pulled out an hour ago.
Not a child's smell anymore, but a young man's air
of college nights and long wool coats
and jokes so cool they cannot be explained.
"You had to be there, Dad," he says.

Now in his scented wake I wait,
knowing he'll soon be gone for good,
graduating to some new city,
paying too much rent.
And this room where for years he slept
and read, while brown hair broke through
on his face and chest . . . Soon
it will be a place for someone else to rest.
But not quite yet.

This fragrant air is sweet to me
tonight. The dusty heat rising
from baseboard vents. The windows tight.
His house-warmed high school books
upright in their case.
Like me, they've done their work.
What we instructors had to say
has all been said. And what he took to heart
is as unfathomable now
as what he cast away.

For he's moving on and on his own
to worlds he'll live to see
but I will never fully know. Of course
he'll stop again to sleep and eat.
We'll speak again of Charlemagne
and Russell Crowe. But the being of him,
that second self housed for years
nearly inside my skin, is elsewhere
flowing on, flown.

How does a father live, I wonder.
But it's late now. At the stair
my wife is calling. And so I remember
that morning my son was first handed to me,
still blood-smudged and birth-slippery.
And because I was a new father then
and because my inexperience showed
the midwife taught me how to hold a child properly.
"Lightly now," she cautioned.
But also pulling at my arms, testing me,
until I sensed what it meant
not to let go.

II

Our Villanelle

Because I loved you more than I could say
and desire was simple from the start
I always thought our troubles would go away.

Green-eyed. Frail-eyed. Grave yet gay.
Your every word rang marvelous and smart
because I loved you more than I could say.

Our bed was nearly perfect in its narrow way.
We touched. We dreamed. We woke a breath apart.
I always thought our troubles would go away.

We had our years. Seasons. A sad last decade.
Denial I practiced as a healing art
because I loved you more than I could say.

The yellow pills are round. The capsules gray.
Minds change, the doctors claim. Why not the heart?
I always thought our troubles would go away.

So life went on. And almost every day
the billowed clouds would gloom before they'd part.
You asked. And because I loved you more than I could say
I left. Your troubles stayed. Mine, I took away.

This Wreck

And yes, to answer your first question
that old car is my car in the front yard
with its three stained hubcaps
and weeds growing up around the soft tires
and a bird-shit spattered hood
that last fall's leaves have worked under.

And yes, it was a well-polished maroon
when I bought it those years ago
a time I remember my wife being pregnant again
and wanting a reliable car
that wouldn't break down during labor
or on the way to the hospital. Or as it happened
on that unforeseen third morning of her life
when we drove our daughter away from home
after midnight blanketed in her new blue car seat
running a funny little newborn fever
her doctor cleared his telephone voice about
before saying he'd be waiting
in the emergency room when we came in.

And yes, he was there in his brown cardigan
after we made the harrowing five mile drive.
And he stayed with us in the brilliant examining room
as specialists appeared in their coats
and the one upholding a spinal tap syringe
seeing my face suggested we'd all be better off
if I waited in the next room.

And yes, there followed some weeks
cut off at the knees and stunned cigarette hours
in the unforgettable hospital parking garage
before being hauled off like freight to my next stop
by gasoline exploding in the cylinders.

And yes, fortunately the meningitis was caught early.
And she was a lucky girl the doctors said
and we were all lucky then and now
that she's better than o.k. with her dancing
and her clean brown hair pinned up in a bun.

And yes, you can understand how sometimes
these high summer evenings home late from work
I open all four doors of the old car
until the steaming inside swollen air escapes.
And settling into one broken seat or another
I look out through the chipped windshield
inhaling the stale sour wonderful
sun-blasted upholstery smell. And then I try thinking
of nothing but roadmaps baking safely in the glove-box
and ballet shoes being tied by small fingers
and nobody going anywhere ever again
in this wreck that will stay in my yard
thank you dear God
for as long as the rest of this takes.

Harvest

The leaves on this leggy shrub
along the garden wall aren't quick
to turn this year. October
slowly eats their edges yellow
then brown. Lately, a spider has found
three well-extended stems
to stretch his iridescent web.
How obvious the gleaming net will be
when all the foliage's gone.

Deep Autumn. Season of gravity,
of waiting, of weightless dreams.
By now the faded lawns
are finished growing. The children's
skins turn white. In the woods
each hunter with a hungry gun
adjusts his sight
to fallen angles of the sun
and shadows on the rise.

It will be colder soon.
The pumpkins know it
lying in the fields. At noon
their mellow, fruitful bodies
still safely stemmed to earth
appear to drowse in season-ending glow.
But all along, seed-deep within
they steel themselves
against the harvest
the flesh being carved.

Winter Hill

If you could watch with me the winter melt
down the long face of my neighbor's sledding hill

you'd see it melting first where children knelt
and slid and trampled trails a month ago.

This February slope, once packed and slick as glass
now drips with footprints by the hundreds

and half-a-dozen spreading stripes of grass
the longer days have finally melted through.

The paper warns it's just an early thaw. Still
this sight of old depressions sunning in the snow

refreshes for this hour—as nature sometimes will—
a view in me I thought would never green.

We know our hopes by light and season, like any slope
or greening thing. Sometimes they trick us.

But why complain. We're made to wait on hope
as every winter hill is made to wait for spring.

Blessed Are Those Who Remember

On a city street, beneath budding trees
two lawyers laugh, tell stories.

The blue-suited one I know. His daughter,
an only child, died one winter

while studying abroad. In the month
it took to ship the body home

his hair turned perfectly white. Now
he calls to me in passing. Tomorrow

or the next day we'll see blossoms overhead.
Blessed are those who can forget.

Labor Day

Not a single cloud all day.
The steep sky a deep blue.
The air perfectly dry. All morning
I worked in the yard, feeling strong
in work boots and leather gloves.
Through the kitchen window
I could see my wife baking. The children
played ping pong on the lawn.
With haircuts and new clothes
they were ready for school.

Later, when the others drove to the lake
I stayed behind in the garden.
The breeze that had blown all day
was still blowing. Bumblebees
moved flower to flower.
Perhaps an hour went by.
I was thinking about my death. Money
and who would miss me. What they might say
on holidays and anniversaries.
How the conversation would go on.

Over the house the sun was dropping.
A line of shade advanced toward me
up the walk. It was moving over flowers,
darkening the colors
as it traveled through the beds.
I could've moved my chair.
But one thought led to another
and only after it happened did I realize
the shadow had reached me.

China

Some people fear big dogs
because they never owned one.

Others dread snow because a teacher
once explained that white isn't a color.

And there are those afraid of books
because of numbers increasing with the pages.

Or China because of the darkness
of strong tea and its many hungry people.

My heart goes out
to those who fear nothing.

In my own house, I often shut these doors
and pull down every shade

against the hour ahead and tomorrow.
Then I consider yesterday

and those I love. What's changed
and what hasn't. What mustn't.

Mrs. Miller

And to the south lived dear old Mrs. Miller,
the first next door neighbor I really knew.
A doctor's widow. White-streaked, yellow hair.
With a nervous New York way of talking
though she'd lived out West for twenty years.

A grown daughter—Dorothy—lived with her,
worked somewhere, drove a red sports car.
Fruit trees grew behind their gabled house
and a crunching path of white crushed stone
ended at a Japanese-style fishpond.

I was tall enough then to climb the bamboo fence
and pull oranges from the tree that overhung
their pond. What fruit I couldn't reach, fell.
In January, you'd see lazy, blurred goldfish
tailing beneath navels floating on the pond.

Saturdays, I'd wash Mrs. Miller's Buick
with a bucket, soap and sponge. The fifteen cents
she paid was good money in '61. Later, on the lanai,
she'd pour my coke, wave away her cigarette smoke,
and engage me in grown-up conversation.

"Since nothing ever goes according to plan," she'd say,
"You'd think we'd figure out the plan."
I was at most eleven. She was a drunk, I suppose.
Confused, but open-hearted. Lonely, of course.
The first person like me I'd known.

Cold

Past fifty, a man longs
for the cold of childhood.
Not these melted winter nights . . .
Gray gutterslush
and sleet crawling down the glass.
With age a man prays
for the true cold he once dreaded.
The uncracked bluing ice.
The snowdrift's pure powder.
The thin blankets and rough arms
and unreliable loves
and how they warmed him.

This is (How) Today

This is how it happened.
A barbecued afternoon. A neighborhood
of bicycles, unfamiliar music, old smoke.
And a man out walking past houses
where mostly brown dogs go bark, bark, bark.
At him! This mostly harmless man
walking the chalk-marked sidewalks.

Today, he feels like barking back.
The polite little houses
are now talking about him
to their mostly brown dogs.
Can this be (he wonders) how a man passes?
Walking. Barked at. Feeling like barking.
Listening to little houses talking.

Crying Man

At O'Hare, after a first jump west to California,
I thought my father was dying, as I waited

for the connecting flight. Being hungry
I ate pizza with the people eating pizza.

Feeling uninformed, I bought newspapers,
opened magazines at a bookshop wall.

Near my gate, I pretended not to watch
a dozen others waiting, as they pretended

not to watch me. But finally, in a hectic airport
restroom, I heard the crying man in his stall.

"Oh God," he cried, behind a stained steel door.
He didn't sound old. And in his privacy, not shy.

"Oh dear God," rang harshly in the close tiled room.
I stood alongside others, a simple traveler

at a public urinal. Behind me the restless waited
their turns. "Oh dear life!" came the third cry.

I shook myself, zipped, found a vacant sink for washing.
Spurting water dwindled to a trickle on my hands.

I lathered and rinsed as I'd been taught. Grabbed
for paper towel. Didn't linger at the mirror.

Beautiful Birds

One day he woke from his nap
and said, "I saw the beautiful birds

and they were singing." At first
he was angry in the wheelchair.

Angry as he once was at me
for defying him. Or as the night

he slapped my drunk brother
after the wreck. Now my father

eats soft food. Wears diapers.
Takes a blood-thinner

that makes his skin bruise easily.
We handle him carefully

as one does a sensitive child
or flowers, nearly gone by.

The Leaves

And at the bend of the autumn road
black birds swarming in morning flocks
and leaves freed from their trees, blowing
dark as birds themselves against a yellow sun.
And I would have said something then
if you'd been with me. Tried again
to make you understand.
The leaves. The birds. The sun.
The leaves.

Five Miles

In the husband's motel room
the toilet flushed by itself
four times in the night.
Even with the bathroom door shut
each flushing woke him
like a whispering in his ear.
Once, out of bed, he pulled back
a weighted curtain on the night.
Street lamps doubled down
the wet city street.
A green truck sleeked by
either very early or very late.
Five miles across town
his daughter slept in her room,
his wife alone in the big bed.
In the morning the man insisted
the toilet could be fixed.
But the manager knew better
gave him a different room instead.

At the Hall's House

There was a house of wood on stilts driven into a hill.
And an old man who cleared the slope and built the house himself
before others came to the valley for snow and raised rich houses
on the hillside. There were books the man wrote as a young man
to pay for the house and a wife and a son and three daughters
who grew up in the valley when the man was strong
and remembered the name of each stranger who entered his house.

And there was a party in the valley a night of the summer.
The decks of the house were cleared as of old and long tables
were laid with cloth and silver. The daughters came home
for the cooking and serving and singing, and the mother
in her beautiful dress was greeting, and the white-headed father
in his tall wooden chair was both recalling and forgetting.
And the guests were poets who ate and talked about dreams
and the blues of the sky and the poems they'd written
and not written that week in the valley. The lamb curries
were green, the baked rice white, and on sideboards
colored wines and red grapes and high salads.

And after the eating was a gathering indoors of the poets
with tables pushed back and the youthful cross-legged on floors.
Then under the one shaded lamp in the big wooden room
a teacher-poet delivered a light poem of thanks,
affectionately rhyming the names and listing the deeds.
Then at her request an elder poet stood and recited
in fine voice a poem of leave-taking from the century past.
Afterwards, many others were moved to recite, and they did
one after another—some smoothly, some stumbling,
some shyly, some boldly, a few voices catching or rising,
most accountably sad. For all in the poems was a week of words
and a night of the heart and a tightening in the room

like laces drawn on a boot until between leather and skin
was no space, no breath, no foreign sensation.

Then a young poet stood, uncertain and for the first time.
Haltingly, she recited a poem about blackberries, its author
on-looking from the side. And his words in her voice
made a strength like an oil that spread in the lamp of the room
until for a time there were no teachers and no students,
no greatness or lack of greatness, no experience dividing
but only light remembered out of life, and feeling recaptured
in such a music of words that briefly among these guests
obstacles to poetry were swept aside. Some felt the move
palpably, as a fragrance or freshness carried into closed space.
In others, the push of words entered like a stream,
redirecting capacities and joining them, lifting into value
failure and grief, answering finally with meaning
and sound's high pleasure such desires as poetry wakens.

For that hour, at least, there seemed no end to them.
No last word. No last poem. And even with the dwindling
a persistence was felt, as the one night broke into many
and lesser streams. So the poets shifted inwardly
recovering surroundings, starting departures. There were scarves
and cloaks and empty glasses. Outside, starlight gapped
through black pines. Looking back on the great front door closing
the guests saw their host in his tall chair dozing. Then down
the steep unlit road home the poets walked in groups and pairs.
Still stirred, of course. But separately now. For some time
off in the near dark, words could be heard and voices talking.

In November

Freely the sky now falls
through bare untroubled trees.
Across my lawn the single leaves blow
brownly west. Some in twos and threes.

At the far stone wall they'll come to rest.
But only until the breezes shift.
Then tumbling and struggling,
a first few winded leaves will lift,

start east again until fencing
stops them, or a hedge.
On Saturday, if it doesn't rain,
I'll rake piles at the wood's edge.

Before dusk I'll drag them in deep.
And if the cares of a man's heart
work the same? I know by now
where the dark trees start.

But tell me, in the open here,
what is at stake?
And where are the tarps?
What do I use for a rake?

The Life

This is the way it was to be.
This is the house where it happened.

This is the room of song and tears.
This is the year he darkened.

This is the word she finally spoke.
This is the tale told the children.

This is the prayer the youngest prayed.
This is the hour God listened.

This is the life that wouldn't last.
This is the reason it didn't.

This is the truth she would accept.
This is the end he couldn't.

The Move

I'd lifted down a few novels, a dictionary.
The first box wasn't yet filled

when my daughter entered the living room.
At sixteen, she was taller than her mother.

But now, at the empty sight of cartons,
small tears started in the corners of her eyes.

Helpless and wordless. Lovingly we stood
among the steady furniture of our lives.

She felt the father moving out of her.
In me, I felt the daughter left behind.

Passage

Before reaching the river
we hear ourselves complaining bitterly
about hot distances,
the insects, our unquenchable thirsts.

Then it's the river we fault.
Too wide to cross safely. The far shore
hidden by low clouds.
We speculate it's really an ocean.

Such hardships we encounter
building our rafts. The splinters
off the rough logs. The thorny
vines tied for lashing.

And how heavy the rafts prove to be
when later, misunderstanding the word
passage, we drag them
across meadows, over mountains.

4/11/02

Now we know that spring will come again
because we're taught it. And by the years, repeatedly.
As in our mixed-up human seasons
even lilacs lighting up a yard
are forgotten once the blossoms fall away.
It's one lesson, though. Like those
our teachers illustrated with solar system overlays
and planets orbiting a blackboard sun.
Remember, as a child, how huge
the seasons felt? And endless seemed the views
our classroom wall of windows framed.
The churning April skies. Ball fields
glowing Easter green. And bursting rows
of wild forsythia, yellow miracles of spring.

But it's coming at us all differently
this year. For myself
I pull a chilly shovel from the shed.
Mornings, I'm out before the garden thaws.
My boot-heel drives a rusty blade
through frost-encrusted earth.
I'm glad the labor's hard.
The wooden handle burns my skin
as I lift and turn and break apart
one wormless chunk of sod
then stab the spade again.
There's something in my early sweat
cut with a dirty smell of clod and upturned stone
that releases in me, temporarily,
the pressure of that other pile
of steel, cement, and bone.

Last rites of winter. First mystery
of spring. A shovel double-digging earth
in the luxury of morning.
Unlike the lilies, we work and pray
for all we're worth, as if without our oversight
the seeds would never germinate,
the trees forget to leaf. Rebirth, some call it.
But among the living this year
it feels unearned, too much up to you and me
to allow it. . .the wildness I mean,
and our fear of it, that keeps us at a distance
or madly digging in,
resisting what can never be resisted.
The towering majesties of grief.
The coming on of spring.

Stalk of Grass

May it be as the saint says
that all will be well
and all manner of things will be well.
But such thoughts don't persist in the mind.
Today at the edge of the meadow

I saw a long grass
that even now, at the height of summer
was a pale, tulip-shoot green.
Reaching out, I let one stalk
run openly through my hand

and briefly felt
that other order of flesh
under my flesh, green to the tasseled end.
But my hand fell back.
And fingering down the stalk

I felt a stickiness, like sap off the green.
Later I found no mark on me.
No residue or trace.
Only this memory of grass
and inside it, my resistance.

Midlife Haiku

Only
so many more times—
the moon and stars

Spent

As for dying, she often said
she didn't mind so very much

except for the expense. My mother
talking about money was my mother

talking about life. The sticky grips
on dad's wheelchair. Odorous

nights when she'd catch the sob
from his rented metal bed, knowing

he'd soiled the sheets again.
No. By expense she meant

not the money drain but how time
went and went until even the clocks

felt empty. Serious in her faith
she'd question me late about

prayers unanswered . . . what it meant
when even her loving God felt spent.

Another Song for My Father

In the morning
before the world wakes
I walk through
damp childhood streets.
It's not just the colors of the houses
that have changed.

These parkway trees
I remember
as mere saplings. Many
I could encircle
with one boy-sized hand.
Today branches
block the sky.

I lean against one.
Stand beneath dying
leaves. Impossible now
to encircle
even the smallest
with my man-sized arms.
I take them in my arms.

Raccoon

August without rain. And these faithful eastern flowers—
cosmos, hollyhocks, black-eyed susans—like the crackled grass
and herbs without a smell, all seem to exhale . . . glad as I am

it's twilight and the sun's slipped behind a hill. From this garden
even the fading sky looks dry. The tall hickories stand like closed
doors, darkening the ends of my yard. Between them, a hurried

sparrow crosses overhead, then an erratic flurry of bats
separately hunting. All this week moles tunneled in the lawn.
And yesterday the cat left a young one's dusty, teardrop body

on the back step. The cat's parched, too. Now she's leaped up
on the birdbath dish. She sips, looks up. Sips again, looks up.
Like a bird, but in slow motion. Here and there, houselights

in the neighborhood are coming on. In the darkening woods
just now I thought I saw the yellow marble of an eye.
Sure enough, a single raccoon appears, formally stepping forth,

overdressed in his stiff, ringed coat. Such an odd, directionless,
halting walk! He sees me and goes up off all fours. The cat sees him
and freezes. The coon notices the cat. In that order. We wait—

poised, uncertain, watching, warm. Then a brightening above
my neighbor's roof: the moon, thirsty and rising!
The cat arches, illuminated in the birdbath. But the raccoon is gone.

At the Lake

Maybe two or three years after
the first child and his wife's shape
better than ever really.
Such a ripeness over ripples
as she wades out from shore.
He can't yet see how she does it.
Not from his spot on the sand.
She figures too large in his heart still.
What he sees is the red bathing suit
hiked high on her legs, the hunching
bladed shoulders, tucked hair
dark as trees on the far shore.
For now, the tie remains inviolate
even as her body arches forward,
diving out into the lake,
resurfacing as a breaking of arms
over green and silvery distances.
"Just once," he will say, years later
when a stranger on a plane asks
if he ever married. He even tries
to describe that day. The pines.
The summer air. Love's feeling
near the end of its beginning.

Blue for Oceans

Astonishing that he could forget and forget and remember so.
California for example. The trees for some reason especially.

Leaving but not losing them. Believing he never would.
Then one day finding March and April gone without a thought

for the peeling eucalyptus, the palms leaning long avenues
the hazy, sky-backed timberlines of the Coast Range.

Years later in a stucco house outside Rome he woke again
to the same yellow-brown light, the dry tile roofs. But the trees

were wrong. Pointed cedars, not aspen or Santa Rosa plum.
Groves of olives, not redwoods. Afterwards, the last clear time

was an evening with his daughter, making a map of the world
out of clay, painting in brown for mountains and blue for oceans,

reading about the scientist who first claimed Africa and America
were once joined. On each side, long-ago animals and jungle birds

watched from trees as a last narrowing isthmus washed away.
For some time after, the gap remained a slight stream

easily forded or even leaped across, one continent to another.
Then years widened the strait and far shores fell away

until only a gull or a seed on a great wind
could cross over the space that was once a world.

Thanks and Acknowledgements

Many thanks to the editors of the following publications in which some of these poems appeared: *Frogpond, New York Quarterly, Concho River Review, US Catholic, Wisconsin Review, Urthona Magazine, Meridian Anthology, Connecticut Review, Roger, Willow Review, Mad Poets Review, New Haven Review, Roanoke Review, Georgetown Review, Pearl,* and *U.S. 1 Worksheets.*

I am very grateful to David Dodd Lee for help with this manuscript.

And my special thanks to the following friends, teachers, editors and places for inspiration and encouragement: Bill Smith, Elizabeth Alexander, Molly Fisk, April Bernard, Donald Sheehan, Dulcy Brainard, Marilyn Krepf, Penelope Laurens, Betty Lies, Ron Padgett, Mark Oppenheimer, Galway Kinnell, Squaw Valley, California, Muffie Locke, Fred Marchant, Brian Slattery, Bob Thompson, Franconia, New Hampshire.